CONSTELLATIONS FOR KIDS

THE FUN WAY TO LEARN ABOUT THE STARS,
DISCOVER THE MAGIC OF THE SOLAR SYSTEM,
AND STARGAZE LIKE AN ASTRONOMER!

ANIELA PUBLICATIONS

CONTENTS

1. WELCOME TO THE AMAZING WORLD OF
CONSTELLATIONS!   1
The Amazing Universe   3
What is a Constellation?   5
Constellations in Different Cultures   6

2. DID YOU KNOW THE STARS LOOK DIFFERENT
FROM DIFFERENT COUNTRIES?   7
A Line Round the Middle of the Earth   8
Hold on Tight—The Earth is Spinning!   8
What Else Is in Our Solar System?   10
The Sun   10
The Moon   12
The Planets   14
Shooting Stars   15
Satellites   17

3. OUR GALAXY, THE MILKY WAY   19
Stargazing and the Solar System: Marvel at the
Night Sky!   21
Welcome to the Solar System   21
Meet the Planets   21
No Telescope? No Problem!   25
The Big Dipper   27
The Tale of Ursa Major and Ursa Minor   29
A Handy Tip From Astronomers   30
Polaris or the North Star   31
Finding North   32
First Stars to Spot   33

4. CONSTELLATIONS FOR SPRING TIME   35
   Cancer   36
   Leo   38
   The Tale of Leo the Lion   40
   Boötes   41
   Virgo   43

5. CONSTELLATIONS FOR SUMMER TIME   46
   Hercules   47
   The Tale of Hercules   49
   Libra   50
   Corona Borealis   52
   Lyra   54
   The Tale of Lyra the Harp   55
   Scorpius   57
   The Tale of Scorpius the Scorpion   59
   Cygnus   60
   Aquila   62
   Sagittarius   64
   The Tale of Sagittarius   66

6. CONSTELLATIONS FOR FALL TIME   67
   Pegasus   68
   The Tale of Pegasus the Winged Horse   69
   Capricorn   71
   Aquarius   73
   Cassiopeia   75
   Aries   77
   Pisces   79

7. CONSTELLATIONS FOR WINTER TIME   81
   Taurus   82
   The Tale of Taurus the Bull   84
   Orion   85
   The Tale behind Orion   86
   Gemini   88

The Tale of Gemini   90
Canis Major   91

8. INCREDIBLE EVENTS IN THE SKY!   93
Comets   94
Meteor Showers   96
Here are some famous meteor showers: 98
Total Eclipse of the Moon   99

9. DID YOU KNOW HOW AMAZING THE
MOON IS?   101
Where Did the Moon Come From?   102
Moon Mice? Absolute Luna-sea!   102
Craters   104
Mountains   104
Maria   105
Lunar Phases and Orbits   106
Moon Visitors   109

Conclusion   111
Glossary   113
Your Feedback is Valued!   115

CHAPTER 1
WELCOME TO THE AMAZING WORLD OF CONSTELLATIONS!

CHAPTER 1

Have you ever looked up at the night sky and imagined what might be out there? You're not alone! People have been wondering that for thousands of years. Technology like telescopes and space shuttles are quite new, so before we could really investigate space, people would make up stories about what they thought was up there.

Some people saw heroes and monsters made out of stars and would tell stories about them. We can see those same pictures today because nothing in space changes very quickly. This book is going to tell you all about the wonderful things floating around above your head and teach you how to find some of the planets and special stars from your bedroom window.

THE AMAZING UNIVERSE

The universe is a really big place. It has to be because everything that exists is inside of it! Our planet Earth is only one very tiny part of it. The universe includes the whole of space with all the stars, moons, and planets, and we can only see the ones that are closest to us. Did you know that the universe is still getting bigger? It is growing so quickly that no one will ever be able to get to the edge.

Inside the universe are billions of galaxies made up of stars, dust, and planets. There are more stars in the universe than anything else. Did you know there are more stars than grains of sand on all the beaches on Earth? Stars have fascinated people for thousands of years. The Ancient Greeks used to believe that if you wished on a shooting star, your wish would come true. Have you ever wished on a star?

WHAT IS A CONSTELLATION?

A constellation is a group of stars that form a pattern. Astronomers used imaginary lines to join stars together into shapes, people, and animals. Often these constellations were named after characters in stories like Hercules, Pegasus, and Orion. You might not have heard of them, but they were very famous to the Ancient Greeks and Romans. The largest constellation is called Hydra and looks like a long sea serpent swimming through the sky.

. . .

There are 88 official constellations, and they can be seen from all around the world. Some constellations have smaller patterns inside them called asterisms. The most famous asterism is the Big Dipper which is part of a constellation called Ursa Major.

CONSTELLATIONS IN DIFFERENT CULTURES

Did you know that explorers have found cave paintings showing pictures in the stars? This shows that even cavemen were using their imaginations when thinking about space and what they could see up there. What is really amazing is that people from different countries looked at the stars and saw very similar patterns.

There is a constellation that the Ancient Greeks called Orion. They made up a story about him chasing seven sisters. All the way over in Australia, the Aboriginal people saw the same stars and also told a story about a man chasing seven sisters, but they called him Baiame.

CHAPTER 2
DID YOU KNOW THE STARS LOOK DIFFERENT FROM DIFFERENT COUNTRIES?

If you stand in front of your house, you will see one view of the front door and porch, and if you stand in the back, you will see another view of the back of the house. It's the same with stars.

Because the Earth is round, it is impossible for people on different sides of it to see the same stars at the same time. There are some stars you can see from Canada that will never be seen from Australia.

A LINE ROUND THE MIDDLE OF THE EARTH

The Earth is split into two halves by an imaginary line around its middle. This line is a bit like a belt, and it is called the equator. All the countries and oceans above the equator are in the northern hemisphere. All the countries and oceans below it are in the southern hemisphere.

The northern hemisphere and southern hemisphere never swap over. One is always on the top, and the other is always on the bottom. The constellations mentioned in this book can all be seen from the northern hemisphere.

HOLD ON TIGHT—THE EARTH IS SPINNING!

The Earth also has an imaginary line called an axis going straight through the middle. Imagine sticking a pencil through an orange. That's what the Earth's axis would look like if we could see it! At the top is the North Pole, and at the bottom is the South Pole.

. . .

This axis is important because the Earth turns around it. This is how we get night and day. It's daytime when your country is facing the sun and nighttime when it is turned away from the sun. As the Earth spins around, you can see different stars, and the constellations will appear in different places in the sky. Knowing where they should be at each time of the year is what helped explorers find their way.

WHAT ELSE IS IN OUR SOLAR SYSTEM?

THE SUN

The sun is our closest star, but it is still 147 million kilometers away. It provides us with all our light and heat, and if we didn't have the sun, then we wouldn't be able to survive. It might look quite small up in the sky, but the sun is actually so huge that you could fit one million copies of the Earth inside it!

· · ·

We've already said that the Earth spins around its axis, but did you know the Earth also spins around the sun? The path that it takes is called an orbit, and the Earth takes one year to go all the way around the sun and get back to where it started. The Earth's orbit isn't a perfect circle; sometimes, it is closer to the sun, and sometimes it is a little further away. This is why we get summer and winter seasons and why the temperature on Earth changes.

THE MOON

The moon orbits the Earth just like the Earth orbits the sun. It takes 28 days for the moon to go all the way around the Earth. Our moon is one out of more than 200 moons in our solar system. Some other planets have more than one moon. Jupiter, the largest planet, has 80 moons!

You can see the moon at night, but it doesn't give out its own light like the stars do. Instead, we can see the moon because the light from the sun shines on it, and the moon reflects this light down to Earth. Over a month, the moon appears to change shape from a full moon to a crescent moon and back again, but that's actually the shadow from the Earth getting in the way of the sun's light.

The moon is about 384,400 kilometers away from Earth, which doesn't sound very close, but it is actually close enough for us to feel the moon's gravity. The moon's gravity pulls things towards it. It isn't strong enough to move the whole planet Earth, but it does make waves on the ocean and pull the tides in and out.

THE PLANETS

There are eight planets in our solar system, and they all orbit around the same sun. The closest planet to the sun is called Mercury. Next is Venus, then Earth, Mars, Jupiter, Saturn, Uranus, and Neptune. All planets are named after Roman gods except for ours. Some of the planets are made out of rock, like Earth, and others are balls of gas.

Like the moon, light reflects off the planets, and you can see some of them from Earth, even without a telescope! The planets that we can see are Mercury, Venus, Mars, Jupiter, and Saturn.

SHOOTING STARS

Seeing a shooting star can be really exciting. Ancient people used to think they were signs that the gods were listening to their prayers. Thanks to scientists investigating, we now know that shooting stars aren't stars at all. They are actually meteors which are small pieces of dust or rock. When they touch the Earth's atmosphere, they heat up and start to glow. Sometimes you can see meteor showers that can last for days or weeks, and there will be thousands of shooting stars in the sky. The best shower is called the Perseids (pronounced per-see-ids), and it happens every August. You can see a meteor every minute!

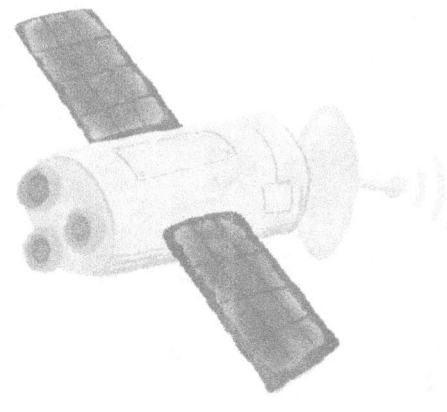

SATELLITES

Not everything in space is natural. There are loads of things that humans have sent up there. If you see a slowly moving star in the sky, it is probably a satellite. Satellites are electronic machines that orbit around the Earth. We use them to send messages around the world, take pictures of the Earth, and check on the weather.

Have your parents got a GPS system in the car or on their phones? There are more than 30 satellites that are used to help people navigate the roads. So next time you see yourself moving on a map, you'll know it's a message sent all the way from space!

CHAPTER 3
OUR GALAXY, THE MILKY WAY

Our solar system is part of a galaxy called the Milky Way. Do you know how it got its name? Roman astronomers looked at the sky and saw a white streak that looked like someone had spilled milk on the stars, so they called it the Milky Way. The Milky Way is home to hundreds of billions of stars and their planets. Everything you can see in the sky is part of our galaxy. There are billions of galaxies in the universe, but ours is the only one that shares its name with a chocolate bar!

STARGAZING AND THE SOLAR SYSTEM: MARVEL AT THE NIGHT SKY!

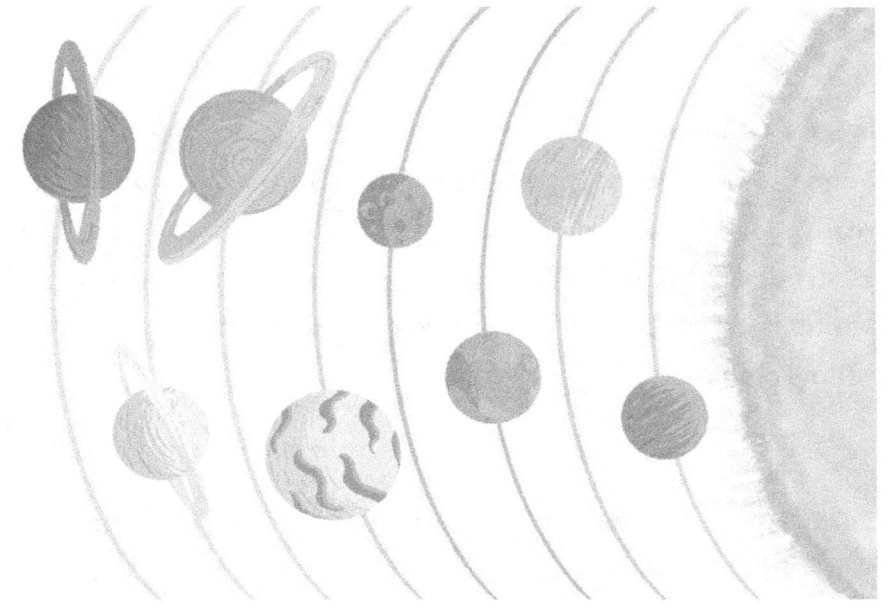

WELCOME TO THE SOLAR SYSTEM

Our solar system is everything that orbits our sun and all the stars, comets, and asteroids that are held in place by its gravity. It's called the solar system because "sol" is an old word for "sun."

MEET THE PLANETS

Mercury is the closest planet to the sun. It is also the smallest planet in the solar system—about one-third as big as Earth.

Days on Mercury are very, very hot, but the nights there are extremely cold. Mercury doesn't have any moons, but it does look a lot like our moon because its surface is covered with craters.

Venus is the second planet from the sun. It spins on its axis really slowly, which means that one day on Venus lasts as long as 243 days on Earth. That's nearly 6,000 hours! The surface of Venus is covered with inactive volcanoes, and its sky is full of yellow clouds.

Earth is the only planet in our solar system that has anything living on it. The other planets are either too hot or too cold. Scientists have spent years looking for signs of life on other planets, but they haven't found anything yet. Aliens must be very good at hide-and-seek!

Mars is known as the "red planet" because it is covered in rusty iron dust. It has volcanoes like Venus, but they are inactive and don't work anymore. Mars has two moons called Phobos and Deimos. There may not be any aliens on Mars, but there are a lot of robots! This is because scientists have been sending them to investigate Mars since 1965.

. . .

Jupiter is the largest planet in our solar system. It is sometimes called a gas giant because it is almost entirely made of gas. The surface is very windy and full of storms. One of these storms makes a swirling red spot that looks like the planet's eye. It makes Jupiter one of the most easily recognizable planets.

Saturn—another gas giant—has the most moons out of all the planets in our solar system: 82! It is also surrounded by rings made up of rocks and ice. These rings are very beautiful and make Saturn the most unique planet to look at. You can see Saturn's rings from Earth if you use a telescope.

Uranus also has rings, but they are much thinner and less bright than Saturn's. Uranus is an ice giant because it is so cold that some of the gasses in its atmosphere have frozen. Uranus is the only planet that spins on its side. Scientists think this is because it was hit by another planet and knocked over!

Neptune is the furthest planet in our solar system and another ice giant. It is a bright shade of blue because of the types of gases in its atmosphere. Neptune is so far away that only one spacecraft has managed to reach it. This distance makes it diffi-cult for us to know as much about Neptune as we do about closer planets. This means there are still lots of things for scientists to discover.

NO TELESCOPE? NO PROBLEM!

There are lots of things you can see in the night sky without any special equipment. In fact, the first astronomers didn't have anything special to help them. They only had their eyes to see and their hands to measure distances.

The easiest thing to see at night is the moon because it is the brightest object and the nearest. At the beginning of the night, it will be in the east. Because the Earth is spinning, the moon looks like it is moving across the sky, so as the time gets later, the moon will move above you and start to set in the west.

The second brightest object in the sky is the planet Venus. You can also see Mercury, Mars, Jupiter, and Saturn. Mars is easy to spot because it looks a little bit red, and Saturn looks a bit yellow.

You can also see thousands of stars in the sky, and you won't need a telescope to find the constellations. In the next few chapters, you'll find out where they are, what they look like, and how to find them.

One of the most exciting things you can see without a telescope is the International Space Station! This is where astronauts live when they are in space. You can see it moving in the sky just after sunset. The light from the sun reflects off the space station's solar panels and makes it the third brightest object in the night sky. To see when the International Space Station is next passing near you, go to spotthestation.nasa.gov.

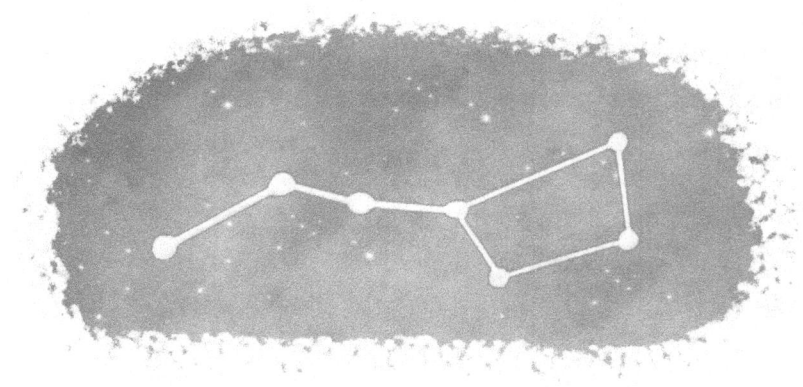

THE BIG DIPPER

Also known as the Plough and the Wagon, the Big Dipper is one of the easiest patterns to find in the night sky. It looks a bit like a saucepan and is made up of seven stars; four in 'the bowl' and three in 'the handle.' The brightest star in the Big Dipper is more than 100 times brighter than our sun, but it's very far away. Nearby is the Little Dipper, a smaller version that is almost the same shape.

Sailors used to use the Big Dipper to navigate at night because it points towards the North Star. Find the two stars at the end of 'the bowl' (these are the two stars furthest to the right in the Big Dipper picture) and draw an imaginary line straight upward through them. Follow that line upward, and you will find a very bright star at the end of the handle of the Little Dipper. These two stars are called the pointer stars because they point to Polaris. Another name for the Big Dipper is Ursa Major, and another name for the Little Dipper is Ursa Minor.

THE TALE OF URSA MAJOR AND URSA MINOR

This epic tale starts with Callisto, a human woman who Zeus's wife, Hera, did not favor. Hera turned poor Callisto into a big grizzly bear. Callisto couldn't go back home to her family and had to live in the woods. Callisto had a son, and she missed him very much. One day, her son went hunting in the woods, and Callisto spotted him from afar. This made her so happy that she ran towards him to give him a big hug, but her son thought she was an ordinary bear coming to attack him! He held up his spear, ready to attack the scary bear.

Zeus was watching all of this from the sky and decided he would help. He picked up Callisto and her son and put them into the stars, where they could always be together. Callisto is Ursa Major—the big bear, and her son is Ursa Minor—the little bear.

A HANDY TIP FROM ASTRONOMERS

Astronomers use a measurement called degrees to show how far apart different objects in space are. You can use them, too, with this amazing trick. All you need is your own hand!

Straighten your arm out in front of you and make your hand into a fist. The distance from your first knuckle (don't count the thumb) to your fourth knuckle is 10 degrees. Now spread out just your thumb and pinkie finger. The distance from tip to tip is 25 degrees. And if you hold up just your pinkie finger, the width of it is 1 degree.

. . .

This handy tip can help you to find the stars. Try it out with Polaris (AKA the North Star)! It should be 30 degrees from the end of the Big Dipper. You can measure this using three fists. Did it work?

POLARIS OR THE NORTH STAR

Polaris is the last star in the Little Dipper, and it is the most important star—apart from our own sun—because it helps us find where north is. Explorers and sailors would use Polaris to make sure they didn't get lost. It is the only star in the sky that doesn't move. In fact, all the other stars look like they're spinning around the North Star.

Polaris is about 70 million years old, which means that some of the dinosaurs would have been able to see it!

FINDING NORTH

You've already learned how to find the Polaris (North Star), but there is another way to find where north is. You can use a compass. Compasses have a needle in the middle that always points to the North Pole. Hold your compass flat in the palm of your hand. Turn around to face the direction the needle is pointing in. Congratulations, you've found north!

If you don't have a compass, you can download a smartphone app that works the same way. Finding north will help you know where to look to find the constellations. If you are facing north, then you also know that east is to your right, west is to your left, and south is behind you.

FIRST STARS TO SPOT

You can use some stars to help you find others. This is another way that Polaris, the North Star, is really useful. Lots of constellations can be found by measuring a number of degrees from Polaris. You just need to use your compass to know which direction to measure in.

You might now know how to find the Big Dipper and the Little Dipper. Remember to look for them in the north.

· · ·

Another easy constellation to find is Orion. This time you will have to look to the south. Use the hand method to measure roughly 30 degrees above the horizon and look for three bright stars in a line. These stars make up Orion's Belt. His arms stretch above this belt, and his legs stand below.

If you measure about 40 degrees west from Orion's Belt, you will find a cluster of stars called the Pleiades. This group is made up of about 3,000 stars, all twinkling together. They look like someone spilled a bag of diamonds in the sky. The Pleiades is one of the closest star clusters to Earth, which is why it looks so bright.

CHAPTER 4
CONSTELLATIONS FOR SPRING TIME

Because the Earth is always moving around the sun, we can't always see the same stars in the sky. Just like you see different things when you look out of your car window, the scenery in space changes every day, but because the Earth is moving in an orbit, it will always come back to the same place at the same time. Astronomers have been able to create maps of the stars, so we know what we will be able to see at different times of the year.

These constellations can all be seen in the springtime (as long as it's not raining)!

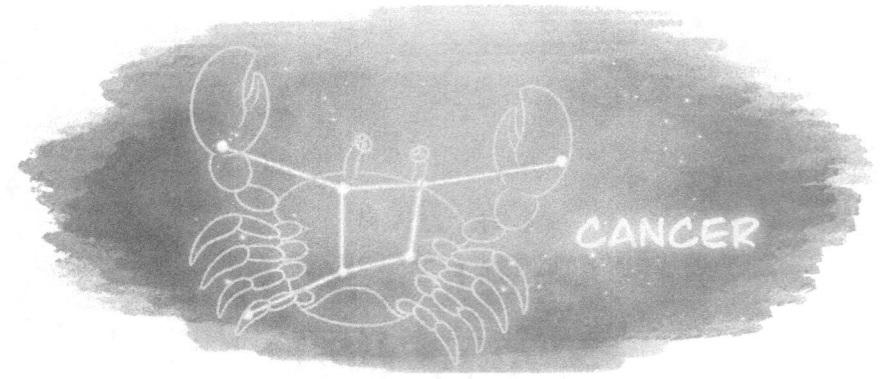

CANCER

The best time to see this crustacean constellation is between February and May. It is quite a hard constellation to spot because the stars within it are not as bright as many others. You will need to remember how to measure degrees with your hands.

First, follow the instructions on the next pages to find the constellation of Leo. Try and imagine a line going along Leo's back, starting with the star at the top of its tail and then joining to the star at the base of its mane. Using your fists to measure 20 degrees, keep drawing that line under Leo's head and out in front of him. You should find the right star in the middle of the crab.

. . .

Another way to find Cancer is to use your compass. Face south and use your fists to measure 50–60 degrees up from the horizon. Depending on the month, you might have to look a little bit more to the left or right. If you combine both of these techniques, you should have a really good chance of spotting it!

Did You Know?

- Cancer was first recorded in 2 AD by a Greek astronomer called Ptolemy.
- This constellation has a star cluster at its center. Called the Beehive Cluster, it has around 1,000 stars and is over 600 million years old.

LEO

Leo, the lion, can be seen roaring across the eastern part of the sky in March, and by May, it's moved to the south. The picture of the lion has been recognized in the sky for more than 6,000 years. It is one of the constellations that are the easiest to see because Leo is made up of some very bright stars.

To find Leo in the sky, you first need to find the Big Dipper. Find the two stars that make up the side of the bowl furthest from the handle. Use your imagination to connect them together and draw a line through them. Keep that line going out of the bottom of the spoon for about 35–40 degrees. Remember, that's three and a half fists! Your line should end at the tip of Leo's tail.

. . .

You can also find Leo using a compass, but the direction you face will change depending on which month it is. In March, face east and measure 40 degrees above the horizon. In April and May, you'll need to measure 60 degrees up and face south to southeast.

Did You Know?

- The constellation of Leo can be seen from both the northern and southern hemispheres.
- Leo is home to 156 different stars, but only 13 of them have been given official names. The brightest star is called Regulus.

THE TALE OF LEO THE LION

Here is a mythological tale that people a long time ago told about the constellation of Leo. The first task given to Hercules involved a lion in the Greek town of Nimea. The lion would go into the town and capture some of the townspeople! When the villagers went to rescue them from the lion's cave, the lion would eat them all up! No one could defeat the lion because its skin was so thick that swords and spears just bounced off it. Hercules fought the lion with his bare hands, defeated it, and freed the captured townspeople.

Zeus's wife, Hera, was upset that the lion had not defeated Hercules, but she wanted to reward it for trying. She put the lion in the stars and made the constellation called Leo.

BOÖTES

There are many different stories about who Boötes was that all come from Greek mythologies. The most famous story tells that Boötes was the man who invented the plough, making farming faster and easier and bringing more food to all the villages. His image was placed in the stars to honor him for his marvelous invention.

If you want to see Boötes for yourself, you'll need to look to the east in April and May, and they turn towards the south in June and July. Don't forget to use a compass or a compass app to make sure you're facing in the right direction. In April, the constellation is only 20 degrees above the horizon, but in the other months, you'll need to measure about 60 degrees.

· · ·

You can also find Boötes by using the Big Dipper to help you. Work out where the handle of the Big Dipper is and join the stars up with a curved line. Keep following that imaginary curve for another 30 degrees, and you should find yourself at the brightest star in Boötes. This star is called Arcturus and is like the belly button of Boötes! Below Arcturus, you can see two legs, and above it is the kite-shaped torso of the plowman.

Did You Know?

- The constellation of Boötes contains 10 stars which have planets orbiting around them.
- There is a huge area of space in Boötes called the Boötes Void because it appears to be empty. It contains 60 galaxies, but in an area that big, you would expect to see around 1,000. That's a lot of missing galaxies! Many astronomers think the Boötes void is pretty spooky because it's so dark. Maybe they're worried something is eating the stars?

VIRGO

The constellation of Virgo is the second largest constellation in the sky. Virgo is usually linked with the harvest and may even be the Greek goddess of the harvest herself. She was called Demeter, and she made sure that the crops grew well and everyone had plenty to eat. Some people think that Virgo is not Demeter but her daughter Persephone who brings about the changes in the seasons. Whoever Virgo is, the constellation shows a young lady holding a sheaf of wheat in her left hand to remind everyone that she brings good health to the crops.

Virgo has some faint stars and some bright stars, which means some parts of the constellation are easier to spot than others. You might have to look really hard to see everything. If you know how to find Boötes, you should also be able to find Virgo.

. . .

Start with the Big Dipper again and imagine a curved line coming out of the handle. Follow that line for 30 degrees—three fists—until you reach the bright star of Arcturus. Keep going for another 30 degrees, and you should find another really bright star. This one is called Spica, and it is the wheat that Virgo is holding.

Another way to find the constellation Virgo is to use a compass to find southeast and measure about 30 degrees above the horizon. Then, look for the bright star of Spica to help you find the rest of the picture. Virgo is best seen between April and June.

Did You Know?

- The constellation of Virgo is home to several galaxies. One of them has been given a really funny name—the Sombrero Galaxy! This is because it is in the shape of a wide hat.
- Spica is a type of star called a blue giant. It is more than 12,000 times brighter than our sun, which is why we can see it from so far away. You should be able to see that it looks bluer than some of the other stars nearby, and this is one way to help you identify it.

CHAPTER 5
CONSTELLATIONS FOR SUMMER TIME

Spotting constellations in summer can be tricky because it doesn't get dark until much later in the day. Of course, the stars are there even in the daytime, but we can't see them because of the light from our sun. The best time to look for constellations is usually about 9:00 p.m., but you might have to stay up even later than that if it isn't dark enough yet!

The good news is that there are plenty of constellations to look for once it does get dark. Here are the summer stars worth missing sleep for.

HERCULES

Hercules is visible in the night sky for five months of the year. In May and June, you can find him due east. In August and September, he will be in the west. And during July, he is right overhead!

The best way to find Hercules is by first spotting two of the brightest stars in the sky. One is Arcturus, the star in the middle of Boötes, and you can check back through this book to remind yourself how to find it. The other star is called Vega. To find Vega, you need to look north-northeast. Draw a line straight up from the horizon to the point right above your head. Vega will be the brightest star on that line.

. . .

Once you've found both Vega and Arcturus, join them up with an imaginary line. Right in the middle of that line should be the Keystone asterism. This is a rhombus of four stars that also acts as Hercules's shorts! You should then be able to also see the arms and legs that make up the rest of the constellation.

You can double-check that you're looking in the right place by measuring from the horizon with your fists. In May and September, measure 3-4 fists. In June and August, measure 5-6 fists. In July, you will need to count out 9 fists.

Did You Know?

- If you have a telescope, you might be able to spot the Great Cluster—a circular group of a million stars. It is on the edge of the Keystone asterism, but even though it has so many stars, it is not very bright.
- There are 29 planets orbiting the stars in Hercules, including a gas giant that is 8 times the size of Jupiter—the largest planet in our solar system.

THE TALE OF HERCULES

The story of Hercules is one of the most famous stories ever told. Hercules's father was Zeus, but his mother was a human woman. Zeus's wife was not happy about this, and she was always doing mean things to Hercules. She made the king send Hercules on 12 impossible tasks, hoping that he would be destroyed. Hercules was very strong and very brave, though, and he finished all his tasks. When he passed away, Zeus made a constellation in his honor. The constellation of Hercules shows him wrestling with the monster Hydra, which was his second task.

LIBRA

The goddess of law in Ancient Greece was called Dike, and she carried a set of weighing scales with her. She would use them to balance up what was fair and just. The constellation of Libra is a picture of those scales, reminding everyone that justice is important.

You can find Libra by facing south in the months of May, June, and July. It always appears pretty low on the horizon, so you'll need to wait until the sun has set fully to be able to see it. Look just above the southern horizon and try to find a bright red star. This star is called Antares. It is between 20–30 degrees up, depending on exactly where you are in the world.

. . .

You will also need to find Spica, the brightest star in Virgo. Once you've spotted both of these stars, try and imagine a line joining them together, and you'll find Libra right in the middle. It's one of the smallest constellations, though, so you might need an expert star-spotter to help you.

Check you're in the right place by measuring 30 degrees above the horizon. There are three stars just above Antares that are in a line like Orion's Belt. Libra is just above those.

Did You Know?

- Libra is the only constellation that gives its name to one of the 12 signs in the zodiac that is not a living creature. All the others are either animals or people.
- The stars of Libra used to be part of the constellation Scorpio. Over the years, they have been recognized as their own constellation but are still very close to Scorpio, and you can use one constellation to help find the other.

CORONA BOREALIS

The Corona Borealis constellation is very small, but because of its shape, it is quite easy to spot. It looks exactly like the object it represents—a shiny, jeweled crown. This crown was given to a princess called Ariadne. It was a wedding present from her husband, the god Dionysus. Dionysus wanted to remember that special day forever, so he made a picture of the crown in the night sky.

You can see Corona Borealis between May and September. It is always near the constellation of Hercules, and you can find it in a similar way. Find the bright stars Vega and Arcturus and imagine a line joining them together. Starting from Arcturus, measure 20 degrees towards Vega, and you should land at another bright star. This is called Alphecca, and it is the brightest star in Corona Borealis. It is at the bottom of the curved crown shape.

Alternatively, you can find Corona Borealis by measuring from the horizon. This can be tricky because it moves around a lot—which is weird, as a crown doesn't have any legs! In May, you need to be facing east and measure 50 degrees (five fists) up from the horizon. In June and July, you need to look more towards the south and measure 70 degrees (seven fists) up from the horizon. In August and September, you should face west and measure at least 30 degrees or three fists.

Did You Know?

- Corona Borealis used to just be called Corona. There is another constellation that looks like a crown called Corona Australis, so the second word was added because people were getting confused. Corona Borealis is the Northern Crown, and Corona Australis is the Southern Crown.
- Corona Borealis only has eight stars in its pattern, and five of them have planets that orbit them.

LYRA

You've probably already seen Lyra but didn't realize it since this is the constellation with Vega in its pattern. Because of this, it is really easy to find Lyra, and you can look for it between the months of June and October. Lyra is actually shaped like a little fish with a triangle tail and a parallelogram body.

Remember how to find Vega? Look to the north-northeast and imagine a line joining the horizon to the highest point in the sky. Vega will be the brightest star on that line. Vega is one of the corners of Lyra's triangle, so if you look around, you should be able to identify the rest of the constellation.

If you'd rather find Lyra by measuring, get your compass or compass app ready. In June and July, you'll need to face east. In

September and October, you'll need to be looking west, but in August, you should find Lyra and Vega right over your head. How many degrees you'll have to measure depends on when you are looking. Because Lyra moves overhead, its distance from the horizon changes quickly. In June and October, measure at least 40 degrees up, but in July and September, you'll need to measure at least 60 degrees.

Did You Know?

- Lyra's brightest star, Vega, was the first star other than our sun to have its photograph taken. Astronomers at Harvard College Observatory did this in 1850.
- Vega is a really important star because it used to be the North Star. Because the Earth rotates on a slight angle, the position of the North Pole changes really, *really* slowly. Eventually, it stopped pointing to Vega and pointed to Polaris again instead. Vega will be the North Star again in about 13,000 years.

THE TALE OF LYRA THE HARP

Not all of the constellations are named after animals or people. Lyra was a harp that belonged to the Greek musician Orpheus. Orpheus traveled with Jason on his quest to find the Golden

Fleece and used his harp to help whenever he could. His music had a magical power to calm angry animals and stop them from being dangerous. Zeus made the constellation Lyra out of stars. It was his way of helping everyone remember Orpheus.

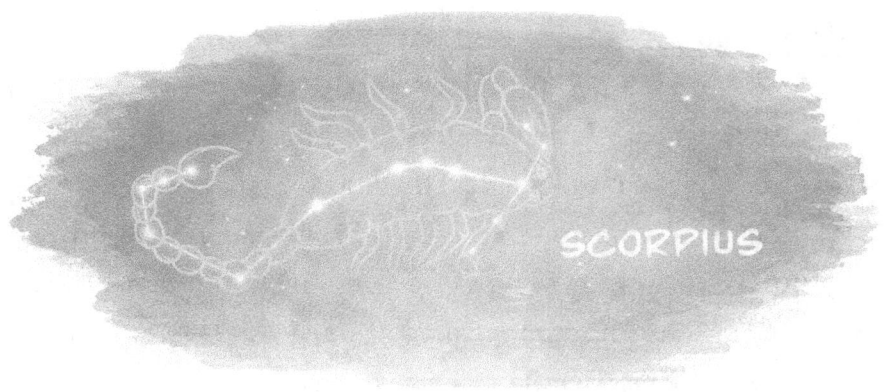

SCORPIUS

This constellation is easier to see if you live in the southern hemisphere, but in the summer, it is possible to spot this sneaky scorpion just peaking over the horizon. You'll have to wait until later in the night to see it, though (around 10:00 p.m.). Your best chance of seeing Scorpius is in July, but you might also be able to spot it in June and August, especially if you live nearer to the equator.

To find Scorpius, face the southern horizon and search for a bright star that looks a little reddish-orange. This is Antares—the same star we used to help us find Libra. On one side of Antares are three stars, all in a line. These make up the claw of the scorpion. On the other side of Antares is a long shape, a bit like a question mark. This is Scorpius's poisonous tail.

. . .

Did You Know?

- In Hawaii, the curved tail of Scorpius is said to represent Maui's magical fish hook. Maui is a demigod who appears in lots of Hawaiian myths, but most people know him now from the film Moana.
- Antares is sometimes called Mars's Rival because the two look very similar. They can be almost impossible to tell apart when they appear in the sky at the same time. Both have a red tint and look brighter than the rest of the stars around them.

THE TALE OF SCORPIUS THE SCORPION

Here is another amazing mythological constellation legend, this time of Scorpius the Scorpion. Orion was such a great hunter that he once boasted he would hunt every animal in the world. This wasn't a very nice thing to say, and the Greek goddess Gaia—who had created all of nature—was very angry with him. She made Scorpius the giant scorpion to protect her animals. Scorpius fought with Orion and managed to defeat him. Zeus was so impressed with Scorpius that he gave him his own spot in the sky as a constellation. There he stayed as a reminder to Orion that it is not a good idea to be boastful.

Orion and Scorpius can never be seen in the sky at the same time. The Greeks said this is because when one appears, he chases the other away. We know now that it is because the Earth is rotating, and the two constellations are at different places in space.

CYGNUS

Later on, you'll discover how the Greek god Zeus changed himself into a bull when he met the princess Europa. However, the constellation Cygnus tells us about another folklore tale where Zeus, again, wanted to get someone's attention by turning into a creature. This time he became a swan, and the person's attention he was trying to get was called Leda, the mother of Castor and Pollux.

Cygnus can be seen flying through the sky between July and October. You'll need to find Vega again, so you must be getting good at this by now! Once you can see Vega, imagine a line that joins it to the northeast horizon. Measure 25 degrees along this line, and you'll pass by the star at the very end of Cygnus's tail. It is called Deneb, and it is also part of an asterism called the

Northern Cross. If you extend the lines of the Northern Cross, you will make two wings and the long neck of the swan.

If you go searching in September, you'll be able to see Cygnus flying right above you. In July and August, you will need to face east and measure 40–70 degrees from the horizon, depending on how early you are looking. In October, you should look west and measure about 60 degrees up from the horizon. Because Cygnus has such a distinctive cross at its center, it is one of the easiest constellations to spot.

Did You Know?

- If you are stargazing from a very dark area, you might be able to see what looks like a thin, milky cloud underneath Cygnus. This is part of the Milky Way, our amazing galaxy.
- If you have binoculars or a telescope, you might also be able to see the North American Nebula. It is a giant cloud of space dust and looks like a faint glow next to the star Deneb.

AQUILA

Another mythological bird in the stars, Aquila, is an eagle that flies close to Cygnus. The eagle belonged to Zeus and was the only other animal apart from Pegasus who could carry his lightning bolts. Aquila was also told by Zeus to bring a human called Ganymede up to Mount Olympus—the home of the gods—to serve them and do all of their chores. Ganymede would eventually be turned into his own constellation called Aquarius.

Aquila can be seen in July, August, September, and October. In July, start by using your compass or compass app to find east and then measure three fists up from the horizon. Face slightly more south in August and look a bit higher—five fists this time. In September and October, you'll have to find the southwestern sky and look between four and five fists above the horizon.

. . .

You can also find Aquila by searching for Vega. Imagine a line going between Vega and the star at the end of the parallelogram of Lyra. Go three fists along this line, and you should see the brightest star at the head of Aquila. This star is called Altair, and it has smaller stars on each side, like little ears.

Did You Know?

- If you join Aquila's bright star, Altair, with Vega and Deneb, you will make another asterism. This asterism is called the Summer Triangle.
- Aquila is the Latin word for eagle, and Altair comes from an Arabic phrase meaning "flying eagle." This constellation has an eagle inside an eagle!

SAGITTARIUS

Sagittarius is another constellation that stays close to the horizon, never getting higher than 20 degrees. This means you'll need it to be very dark outside, and you might only be able to see part of this mythical archer. The only time to see Sagittarius in the northern hemisphere is from July to September.

Face the south and use the tips on the previous pages for finding Altair. Use your fists to measure 40 degrees from Altair to the southwestern horizon. You should now be near a special group of stars in Sagittarius: the Teapot asterism. This asterism is the chest and arms of the archer as he pulls back his bow, ready to fire toward the nearby Scorpius.

. . .

If you want to find Sagittarius using your compass or compass app, you need to find and face south. Measure 10–20 degrees up from the horizon, and keep looking for that teapot shape.

Did You Know?

- Although you can see Sagittarius in the northern hemisphere, it is more commonly thought of as a southern hemisphere constellation. It is actually the largest southern hemisphere constellation but only the 15th largest constellation overall.
- Sagittarius is at the center of the Milky Way galaxy. This explains why there are so many star clusters and nebulae within the constellation.

THE TALE OF SAGITTARIUS

Here is another handed-down legendary tale. The constellation of Sagittarius is supposed to represent Chiron, who was an archer in Greek mythology, but he was extra special because he was also a centaur (a mythological creature). A centaur has the body of a horse, but where the horse's neck should be is the torso, arms, and head of a man. Centaurs were supposed to be very wise, and Chiron was the wisest of them all. He taught many great heroes like Hercules, Jason, and Achilles.

One day there was an accident, and Chiron became really unwell because he was poisoned by the Hydra that Hercules defeated. Even though Chiron was a skilled healer, he couldn't stop the poison from making him unwell. So, Zeus lifted Chiron up and put him in the stars, where he could stay forever and not be sick anymore.

CHAPTER 6
CONSTELLATIONS FOR FALL TIME

As the days start getting shorter, you have longer night times to spend stargazing. The stars that you saw in the spring are now as far away as they can be, and a completely new set of stars twinkle in the sky.

PEGASUS

The mighty winged horse is a good constellation to find. It has an easily recognizable shape, including an asterism in the shape of a square. The neck and head of Pegasus start at one corner of this square from a star called Markab. Two front legs come out of another star called Scheat. You can see Pegasus in the sky from September all the way through to December.

Use your compass to find the eastern horizon, and measure 30 degrees up in September and 60 degrees up in October. You should be able to see the Great Square asterism because the four stars at the corners are very bright. If you're looking in November, remember to face south instead of east and measure 70 degrees up. In December, Pegasus moves all the way round to the west and can be found 50 degrees up.

. . .

You can also find Pegasus if you know where the North Star is. You can find it by locating the Big Dipper and following the pointer stars. Imagine a line from the end of the Big Dipper's handle to Polaris. Measure twice as far again, and you should reach a group of stars that make a W shape. Find the brightest star at the end of this W and draw another line from Polaris that goes through it. This line will take you to the Great Square of Pegasus.

Did You Know?

- Because the Great Square is so easy to spot, it is used by navigators and astronomers to help find other features in space.
- The first planet to be discovered outside our solar system is orbiting a star in Pegasus.

THE TALE OF PEGASUS THE WINGED HORSE

Here is the fable of the mighty Pegasus. Pegasus belonged to a Greek hero called Bellerophon. Together they went on many adventures. Pegasus helped Bellerophon fight a terrible monster called the Chimera. It was part lion, part goat, and part snake, and it breathed fire.

. . .

CHAPTER 6

Pegasus was a very special horse, and not just because it had wings and could fly. If it stamped its hoof on the ground, water would shoot up in a jet, and if Pegasus clapped its wings together like we clap our hands, it would make the sound of thunder. Pegasus was also the only animal that could carry Zeus's lightning bolts without getting hurt. Zeus would often borrow Pegasus to help him out, and he decided to make a constellation to honor Pegasus for being so loyal and helpful.

CAPRICORN

When the Greek philosopher Ptolemy wrote down the stories of all the constellations, he said that Capricorn was the image of the Greek god Pan. Pan was a man with goat's horns and legs. In one story, Pan was being chased by a monster and had to jump into a river to escape. When his legs got wet, they changed into a fish's tail.

The constellation of Capricorn is really difficult to see with just your eyes because the stars that make up this picture are very faint. If you want to catch a glimpse of the mythical half-goat half-fish, you'll need to find somewhere very dark and far away from artificial light. Capricorn is visible between September and November.

. . .

Make sure you're facing south and look for the bright stars Vega and Altair. These stars are in the constellations of Lyra and Aquila. Starting at Altair, imagine a line going through Vega. Measure three fists (30 degrees) from Vega, and you should land on the constellation of Capricorn.

Another way to find Capricorn is to measure 30 degrees up from the southern horizon. Look slightly east in September and slightly west in October.

Did You Know?

- The star in Capricorn's horns called Algedi is actually two stars! These stars orbit each other, and you can see the separate stars with a pair of binoculars.
- Most constellations were first written down by the Ancient Greeks, but Capricorn seems to have been designed by the Babylonians. Ancient relics with pictures of a goat with a fish tail have been found that are 4,000 years old.

AQUARIUS

Remember Ganymede, the young man taken up to Mount Olympus by the eagle Aquila that we talked about earlier? Well, he is the constellation Aquarius. The tale goes that in return for bringing the gods drinks and filling their cups when they were thirsty, Ganymede was promised that he would never get old. Zeus put him up in the stars so that he would always be there.

You can try and spot this constellation between September and November, but it might take a lot of practice because Aquarius doesn't have any bright stars. It is very close to Capricorn and Pisces, so you can use these other constellations to help you.

Like the ancient astronomers, you can use the Great Square of Pegasus to help you find Aquarius. Find the star Scheat, which is the corner of the square with the legs of Pegasus. Draw a line from this star to Markab, the star at the base of Pegasus's neck. Keep that line going through Markab for 20 degrees, and you should land on Aquarius.

You can also find Aquarius by facing south—don't forget to use a compass or compass app to help you. Measure 30 degrees up from the horizon. Look southeast in September and southwest in November to follow Aquarius across the night sky.

Did You Know?

- The name Aquarius comes from the Latin word *aqua,* meaning water. In the stars, Aquarius can be seen pouring water from a jug.
- Aquarius is one of several constellations with a water theme. These are found in an area of space known as "The Sea."

CASSIOPEIA

The fable of Queen Cassiopeia contains Greek Gods and sea monsters! Queen Cassiopeia once boasted that she was even more beautiful than Poseidon's daughters. Poseidon, the Greek god of the sea, was not very happy with her claims and sent a sea serpent to attack her kingdom. After Cassiopeia's defeat, she was placed in the stars as punishment for being so vain. In her constellation, she is chained to a giant throne, and for half the year, she has to hang upside down.

The constellation of Cassiopeia is one of the few constellations that is visible all year round, but the best time to see it is between September and February. Cassiopeia is near the North Star. Find the Big Dipper and draw a line from the pointer stars to Polaris. Keep the line going for the same distance again, and you will land on Cassiopeia. The five stars of Cassiopeia are shaped like a W or M, depending on which way up it is. All five stars are very bright, so they should be easy to spot.

Cassiopeia is found in the northern directions during the fall and winter months, so you can use a compass to make sure you're looking in the right direction. Look to the northeast in September, turn north for November, and northwest in January. The constellation rises and falls overhead, so you'll find it 30–40 degrees high in September and February, rising up to 70 degrees in November.

Did You Know?

- All five of the stars in Cassiopeia have official names. They are Segin, Ruchbah, Gamma, Schedar, and Caph. Schedar looks orange, while all the others appear white.
- The constellation used to be called Cassiopeia's Chair because of the throne she is tied to. The name was only changed in 1930.

ARIES

The mythological tale of Aries states that he was a special ram with a beautiful golden fleece. He was offered as a tribute to Zeus, and Zeus placed the ram in the stars. Aries's Golden Fleece was guarded by a dragon. The hero Jason was sent to recover it.

This constellation is best seen between October and January, and even then, it can be tricky to spot. Look out for the brightest star, Hamal, to help you. Aries is shaped like a straight line with a slight bend on the end, and Hamal is in the middle.

The easiest way to find Aries is to first look for Cassiopeia. Find the two stars called Caph and Shedar. Remember, Shedar is easy to spot because it has a yellow-orange tint. Draw a line between the two and follow it beyond Shedar by 40 degrees. This will take you to the constellation of Aries.

Finding Aries with your compass is harder because it moves a lot between the months. In October, face east and measure 30 degrees up. In November, face southeast and measure 70 degrees up. In December, you'll still measure 70 degrees up, but this time, you need to make sure you're facing south. In January, you will have to face to the west and measure 50 degrees up from the horizon.

<u>**Did You Know?**</u>

- Aries is home to a spiral galaxy that is 450 million light years away from Earth.
- 2,000 years before the Greeks named Aries, the constellation was already imagined to be the shape of a ram by Babylonian astronomers.

PISCES

PISCES

Pisces is the Latin word for fish, and there are two fish in this constellation. The story goes that the constellation represents two fish that saved the goddess Aphrodite and her son Eros when they were being chased by a monster. They jumped into a river to escape, and two fish swam over and helped them to safety.

This is another tricky constellation to spot because there are no bright stars in Pisces. The constellation is a large V shape with a star at the point, which joins the tails of the two fish together. This star is called Alrescha.

The best time to spot Pisces is between October and January. You can use the Great Square to help you find Pisces. If you measure 10 degrees to the east of the Great Square, you should land on one of the fish, and if you measure 10 degrees to the south, you should find the other. Alrescha is 20 degrees to the southeast.

In October, find the eastern horizon with your compass and measure up 30 degrees to find Pisces. Do the same in January but facing west. In November and December, you'll need to face south and measure up 60–70 degrees.

Did You Know?

- Pisces is in the area of the sky known as "The Sea," along with other water-themed constellations like Aquarius and Capricorn.
- Thirteen of the stars in Pisces have their own planets.

CHAPTER 7
CONSTELLATIONS FOR WINTER TIME

Winter isn't always the easiest time to see constellations, which is a shame, as some are only visible during these months. Bad weather means that the skies are often cloudy and the stars are obscured. However, if you do manage to find a clear day, there are some great constellations to spot.

TAURUS

The bull Taurus can be seen rampaging across both the northern and southern hemispheres but at different times of the year. You can see it best between December and March by looking towards the south.

Taurus is very close to the constellation of Orion. If you draw an imaginary line through the stars on Orion's belt and keep following it west for an extra 30 degrees, you will reach the head of the bull. The head is a small triangle with two long horns coming out of the top. If you keep following your line for an extra 10 degrees, you will come to a star cluster called The Pleiades.

. . .

Taurus is lower in the sky in December and March, so you'll need to measure 40–50 degrees from the southern horizon. Look a little to the east in December and January and a little to the west in March. In January and February, you'll have to measure 60–70 degrees up as the stars rise higher.

Did You Know?

- The constellation of Taurus has been drawn as a bull for more than 10,000 years! Pictures of this arrangement have been found in cave paintings.
- Taurus and Orion face each other as if they are in battle. This makes sense because Orion is a great hunter.

THE TALE OF TAURUS THE BULL

In this magical story, Zeus became interested in a human princess called Europa and wanted her to like him too. Because humans can only see gods when they are in disguise, Zeus decided to turn himself into a giant white bull. He went to Europa when she was gathering flowers on the shore. Europa had never seen such a friendly bull before, and she climbed on Zeus's back. He plunged into the sea and swam all the way to the island of Crete with Europa still riding on his back.

Zeus changed into a man and told Europa who he was. She stayed on the island, and they started a family together. Because Zeus was a god, he didn't get older, but Europa did. When she passed away, Zeus was very sad, so he turned into the bull one more time and carried Europa up to the stars, where they became the constellation Taurus the Bull.

ORION

Orion is one of the most famous constellations and is also one of the easiest to spot. The distinctive belt of three bright stars means it can even be seen when the sky is not very dark. Although you can see Orion at many times of the year, the best time to spot the constellation is from January to March.

Finding Orion with a compass is quite easy. Use it to help you find the southern horizon and measure up. In January, you'll have to look slightly to the east and measure 30 degrees. In March, look slightly to the west and measure 40 degrees. In February, the constellation is at its highest, so you will need to measure 50 degrees.

. . .

You can also find Orion without measuring because of how bright Orion's Belt is. Face south and look up until you see three bright stars all in a line. Orion's shoulders rise up from the belt. Look out for the bright star called Betelgeuse in his armpit! Orion's knees are the same distance below the belt, and the bright star on one knee is Rigel.

Did You Know?

- Orion's Belt is an asterism that has been recognized for thousands of years. The Ancient Egyptians designed their pyramids, so they would point to this asterism.
- Underneath Orion's Belt is the Orion Nebula, but you can't see it without using a powerful telescope because it is very far away.

THE TALE BEHIND ORION

This is the old legend of Orion, a hunter who lived with Artemis, the Greek goddess of the forest and wild animals. Orion was a demigod, and his dad was Poseidon, the Greek god of the sea. Orion and Artemis were in love and wanted to get married, but her brother, Apollo, did not want this to happen. He decided to play a trick on Artemis. She was also a very good hunter, and Apollo dared her to fire an arrow and hit a small target in the lake. The lake was very far away. However, Artemis was an excellent shot, and her arrow hit the target.

When she went to see what she had hit, she was upset to see it was Orion, who had been swimming in the lake. Not wanting to forget him, Artemis put his image in the stars, where he is shown with his hunting club held high.

GEMINI

The stars that make up the heads of Castor and Pollux are bright and easy to spot, but being able to see the rest of the constellation Gemini requires a very dark sky because the stars are much fainter. Your best chance to see the celestial twins is between January and April.

First, find Orion's Belt and the neighboring stars Betelgeuse and Rigel. If you imagine a line from Betelgeuse going all the way through Rigel and a further 30 degrees, you should find yourself near two fairly bright stars. Named after the twins, the brighter one is Pollux, and the other is Castor.

If you can't see Orion, you can try and find Gemini by measuring degrees from the horizon. In January, face east and measure 40 degrees high. In February, March, and April, you will need to face roughly south and measure about 60–70 degrees high. Once you have spotted the two twin stars, you should look for two stick figure bodies lying parallel with the brightest stars as the heads.

Did You Know?

- Castor is actually a whole system of 6 stars that are so close together that they look like one star.
- The star Castor looks bluish-white, and Pollux looks yellow-orange. This is how you can tell them apart. Maybe the twins aren't identical after all!

THE TALE OF GEMINI

Gemini's famous legend contains identical twins! The constellation of Gemini is named after Castor and Pollux, twin sons of the Queen of Thebes. They looked absolutely identical; however, Castor's dad was the king, and Pollux's dad was Zeus. This made Pollux immortal, which meant that he could live forever.

Castor and Pollux did everything together, including going on adventures. They helped a hero called Jason to find the golden fleece of Aries the ram. The twins had a sister called Helen, who was the most beautiful woman on Earth. One day, Helen was captured and taken to the city of Troy. Her brothers fought in the war to get her back, but Castor was defeated. Pollux didn't want to keep living without his brother and asked Zeus to bring Castor back.

Even Zeus, the king of the gods, could not bring someone back from defeat in battle, but he reunited the twins by placing them both in the night sky. The constellation Gemini looks like two stick men, each with a star as its head. One star is called Castor, and the other star is called Pollux.

CANIS MAJOR

Canis Major is Latin for "greater dog," and this constellation represents one of Orion's hunting dogs. Canis Major can be seen following Orion around the sky. It also looks like it is chasing another constellation called Lepus, which looks like a rabbit or hare. Canis Major is an important constellation because it is home to the brightest star in the sky: Sirius–sometimes called the "Dog Star."

Canis Major never gets very high in the sky, making it a bit tricky to spot. You can only see it in the northern hemisphere in February, March, and April.

Orion can help you to find Canis Major. Look for Orion's Belt and imagine joining up the three stars. Continue that line towards the southeast and measure two fists or 20 degrees. You should come very close to Sirius, which sits on Canis Major's collar like a shiny tag.

If you face the south and measure 3 fists, or 30 degrees, up from the horizon, you should also find Canis Major. Look a little to the east in February and a little to the west in April.

Did You Know?

- Sirius only looks like the brightest star in the sky because it is so close to Earth—only 8.6 light years away. It doesn't actually shine that brightly compared to some of the other stars.
- There is another "dog" constellation in the sky called Canis Minor, which means "lesser dog" in Latin.

CHAPTER 8
INCREDIBLE EVENTS IN THE SKY!

Now that you know the best times of year to see certain constellations, you might also like to watch out for some of the other exciting things that happen in space.

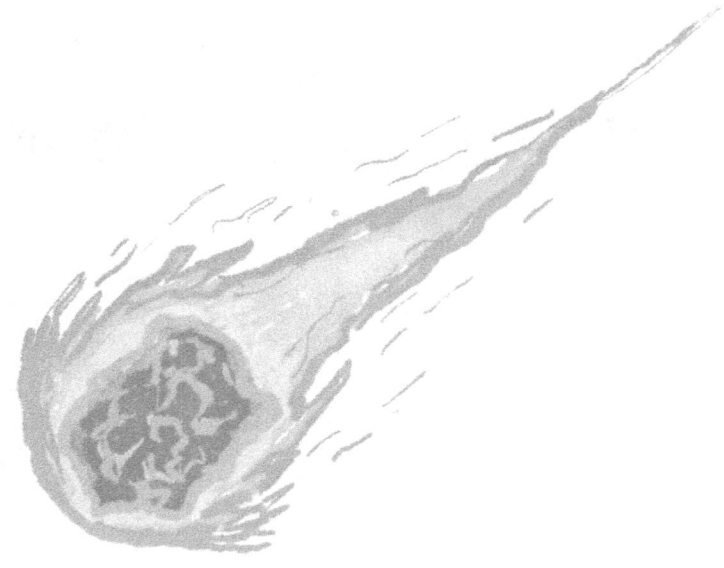

COMETS

Comets orbit the sun just like the planets, but they are much, much smaller. They are mainly made up of ice, but they also have bits of rock and gas in them, too. As they fly around in space, they drop lots of pieces off and leave clouds of space dust. This dust appears like a long, fuzzy tail that trails behind each comet. The head of the comet burns brightly, and most are easy to see using only your eyes.

. . .

Comets take a lot longer to orbit around the sun than we do because they are further away—even further away than Neptune. Some comets take hundreds of years to complete their orbit. The most famous comet is called Halley's Comet, and it takes around 76 years to make one circle of the sun.

When some comets, like Halley's Comet, fly past the Earth, we are able to see them. This doesn't happen very often, which makes it really exciting when one appears. Halley's Comet won't be visible from Earth again until 2061, and many people who saw it in 1986 won't be around to see it again.

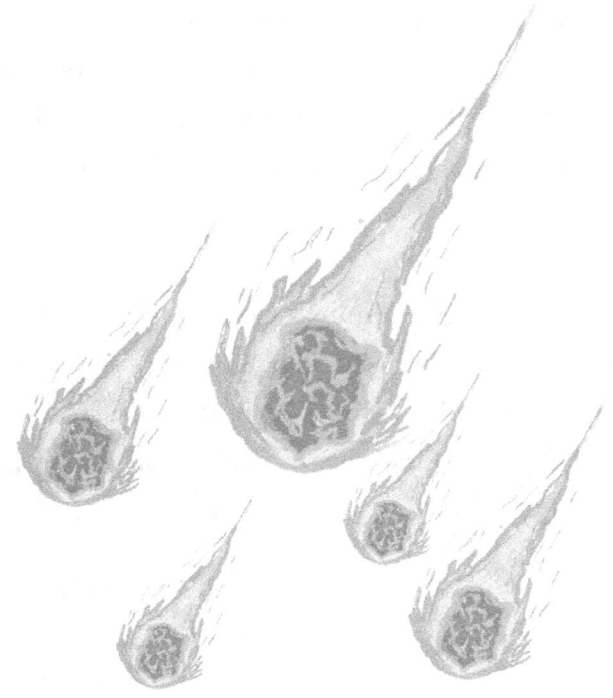

METEOR SHOWERS

You already know that meteors are small pieces of space rock or dust, but I bet you didn't know just how many meteors crash through the Earth's atmosphere every year. Meteor showers are like massive fireworks displays where loads of meteors appear over the course of several days.

. . .

Meteors are created by comets. When the Earth's orbit passes through a stream of space dust left by a comet, the dust and rocks that enter the atmosphere heat up so quickly that they burn brightly and look like shooting stars.

Because the Earth moves through the same clouds of dust every time it goes around the sun, astronomers are able to tell everyone when the meteor showers will happen. There are hundreds of meteors hitting the Earth every day, even when it isn't nighttime, but you'd have to be looking at exactly the right time to spot one.

If you want to watch a meteor shower, check the best days by using a website like timeanddate.com. Find yourself somewhere in the countryside, well away from towns or cities, which give off lots of light. Make sure you have a clear view of the sky, lie down on something comfy, and wait.

HERE ARE SOME FAMOUS METEOR SHOWERS:

- The Quadrantids shower happens in the first two weeks of January every year. At its peak, you can see up to 110 meteors every hour! They originate close to the constellation Boötes, and this is why they are sometimes called the Boötids.

- The Lyrids start near the constellation Lyra, and they happen in the middle of April. You can see them from both the northern and southern hemispheres. You will have to be patient, though, because even on its best days, you probably won't see more than 18 meteors per hour.

- The Perseids meteor shower is the brightest of the year and lasts for most of July and August. The best time to watch is the second week of August when you can see up to 100 meteors streaming across the sky every hour. The Perseids seem to come from the constellation Perseus, but they are actually the cloud of a comet called Swift-Tuttle.

- The Leonids blast out of the constellation Leo every November and are best viewed in the middle of the month. Even then, you will probably only see one meteor every five minutes.

TOTAL ECLIPSE OF THE MOON

The moon is the brightest object in the night sky, so it's pretty hard to miss. Have you ever noticed that the moon changes shape? Sometimes it even disappears altogether. This happens when the Earth gets caught between the sun and the moon, and the light from the sun gets blocked. It only happens during a full moon and usually only twice a year. However, you won't be able to see all the lunar eclipses because they are only visible from certain places on the planet.

There are two types of lunar eclipses. A total lunar eclipse happens when the moon completely disappears for a few minutes. This means that the Earth has entirely blocked the light from the sun. A partial lunar eclipse happens when the Earth isn't completely between the sun and the moon. When this happens, you'll see the shadow pass over the face of the moon like someone is taking a bite out of it.

CHAPTER 9
DID YOU KNOW HOW AMAZING THE MOON IS?

Because the moon is always there, it can be easy to take it for granted, but it's actually really special. The moon is the only natural thing orbiting Earth, and it has been there for 4.6

billion years! That's 1 billion years before the first living things appeared on Earth.

WHERE DID THE MOON COME FROM?

It's very difficult for scientists to know exactly where the moon came from because no one was around to see it first appear. Their best guess is that the moon is actually made of pieces of Earth! Billions of years ago, the Earth was probably hit by a large object the size of a smaller planet. This caused the Earth to break, and bits went flying off into space. The other planet would have been completely broken up, too (like crumbling a cookie), and these bits of dust would have been floating around in space.

Because the Earth has a strong force of gravity, it started to pull these crumbs and rocks together, eventually making the moon. This theory explains why there are rocks, metals, and gasses on the moon that are exactly the same as on Earth.

MOON MICE? ABSOLUTE LUNA-SEA!

Because we can see that the surface of the moon is full of bumps and patches, people used to joke that it was made of cheese! Have you ever seen a slice of Swiss cheese? It is crumbly and full of holes and looks just like the moon, only yellow.

Sadly, the moon is actually made of rock, which is not as tasty. It also has features like the Earth with mountains and seas, and scientists have even given them all names. The most famous is the Sea of Tranquility which is where the astronauts Neil Armstrong and Buzz Aldrin landed when they visited the moon in 1969.

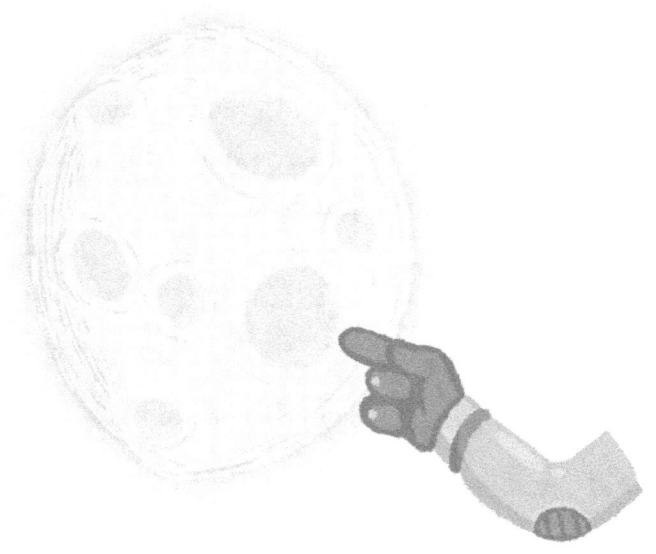

CRATERS

The bumps and holes you can see on the moon are called craters. They are like large bowls, and they make up more than 80% of the moon's surface. Have you ever dropped stones into a sandbox or the sand on the beach? Those stones leave little craters and dips in the sand when they hit it. The craters on the moon were formed when meteors and other space debris crashed into the moon.

MOUNTAINS

In between the moon's craters, you can find some really tall mountains. They were also made by the impact of rocks hitting the moon. When a meteor hits the moon, it pushes the rock and dust out of the way. Some of it gets squashed down, but other bits get shoved to the side of the crater. This makes the sides bigger, and if a lot of rock and dust is pushed to the side, it makes a mountain. The tallest mountain on the moon is called Mons Huygens, and it is 5.5 kilometers tall. This is about the same height as Mount Saint Elias in Alaska.

MARIA

The dark, flat parts of the moon are called the maria, another word for seas. The first astronomers to look at the moon with a telescope thought that these maria looked like they were made of water. However, this turned out to be a mistake because there is no water on the moon.

The maria are flat because they used to be covered in lava. This was probably made in the center of the moon when all the dust and bits of Earth were being pushed together. There is no lava there now. It has cooled down and turned into a type of rock called basalt. Robots have visited the moon and brought some of these basalt rocks back to Earth for scientists to investigate. Scientists are very excited by moon rocks and have collected about 400 kg of samples. That's roughly how much an American crocodile weighs!

LUNAR PHASES AND ORBITS

The moon orbits around the Earth just like all of the planets orbit around the sun. It takes roughly 28 days for the moon to make it all the way around the Earth and back to where it started. The moon also spins on its axis. It takes about 28 days for the moon to make one full rotation. Because it takes the same amount of time for the moon to spin around as it does for it to go around the Earth, the same side of the moon is always facing the planet. This is why, no matter where the moon is in the sky, the pattern on its surface is always the same.

. . .

During its 28-day cycle, the moon changes shape. This happens because the light from the sun hits different parts of the moon. Sometimes the light shines on the side of the moon that we can't see from Earth, and this makes the moon look dark. Try shining a flashlight on an orange, slowly moving the light in a circle around the fruit.

The moon has five different stages in its cycle:

- Full moon: This is when the moon looks completely round, and we can see all sides of the circle.
- Gibbous moon: The moon looks squished on one side as it becomes covered in shadow.
- Quarter moon: Only half of the moon is visible. The rest is dark. Why is it called a quarter moon and not a half moon? Because the other side of the moon— the one facing away from Earth—is also dark. This means the moon has one-quarter in the light and three-quarters in shadow.
- Crescent moon: This is the moon shape we often see in pictures, where it looks like a smile on its side.
- New moon: This is the thinnest slice of the moon, and it is often so dark that we cannot see it by using just our eyes. It only lasts for a day or two, so the moon isn't gone for long.

The moon takes two weeks to go from a full moon to a new moon. When the area of the moon that reflects the sun's light gets smaller, we say that the moon is waning. It takes another two weeks for the moon to go from a new moon back to a full moon. During this time, the shadows covering the moon get smaller, and the lighter side gets larger. We call this the waxing moon.

MOON VISITORS

Because the moon is the nearest space object to Earth, it is the easiest for scientists to send spacecraft to. Some of these rockets have had astronauts in them, some have had robots, and others have just flown close by and taken photos.

Back in the 1950s, both the United States and Russia really wanted to be the first country to land on the moon. They both built a lot of rockets and made new designs that they hoped would be able to make the long journey. This time in history is known as the Space Race.

Russia made the first spacecraft to take a picture of the far side of the moon. They also made the first landing on the moon's surface. Neither of these spacecraft had any people inside, though. They were controlled by pilots back on Earth.

The United States was the first country to send astronauts to the moon. The first spaceship just flew around the moon. It was called Apollo 8. Seven months later, a spacecraft called Apollo 11 successfully landed on the moon, and two astronauts, Neil Armstrong and Buzz Aldrin got out and walked around.

Over the next few years, both countries sent robots to the moon. These robots took photographs and videos and collected rock samples. The newest robot on the moon was put there by the Chinese space program in 2019.

CONCLUSION

Good work! You've unlocked many secrets of the stars and are ready to impress your friends with your knowledge of the constellations. From the giant Virgo to the much smaller Corona Borealis, you know all the tips and tricks to find them as well as some amazing facts that will make you sound like a professional astronomer.

There are 24 constellations mentioned in this book. Have you managed to spot them all? Hopefully, you've had lots of fun learning about the wonderful pictures that ancient civilizations saw in the stars, but your adventures in space don't have to end here. There are 88 constellations in total, and now that you know how to navigate the night skies, you are ready to find the rest. You can use a brilliant app like Stellarium to see all the constellations in the sky all around you.

While you're looking to the stars, don't forget there are plenty of other objects to find as well. Watch out for the different phases of the moon, some planets pretending to be stars, and maybe even a magical meteor shower! There are so many things in space to explore that not even scientists know exactly what is out there. Who knows what they (or you!) will discover in the future? Happy stargazing!

GLOSSARY

Some of the words used in this book might be new to you. You can find out what they mean here.

Asterism: A pattern formed in the night sky by joining stars together. Smaller than a constellation.

    Astronomer: A type of scientist who studies things in space.

Axis: An imaginary line through the middle of something in which an object rotates around.

Constellation: A group of stars that make a pattern. There are 88 official constellations.

Degree: The unit used to measure the size of an angle.

Equator: An imaginary line around the middle of the Earth.

Galaxy: Many stars grouped together by the force of gravity.

Gravity: A force coming from inside a large object which attracts smaller objects towards it.

Hemisphere: Half of the Earth. The equator divides the Earth into the northern and southern hemispheres.

Planet: A large object in space that orbits around a star.

Meteor: A small space rock that enters the Earth's atmosphere and burns up, creating a bright streak.

Nebula: A cloud of dust or gas in space.

Orbit: The path taken by an object moving in a circle or oval around another, larger object.

Star: A ball of gas that gives out its own light. The sun is our nearest star.

YOUR FEEDBACK IS VALUED!

You know what's even "cooler" than the planet Neptune?

What's that?

When we get feedback from awesome readers like you! We'd love it if you would consider leaving an honest review for this book on Amazon or Audible.

Ok, good to know that we can help!

Thank you, and happy stargazing!

As an independent publishing team floating through space, it would mean the UNIVERSE to get your feedback. It will help us create better books for you and help educate other space travelers even more!

Aniela Publications